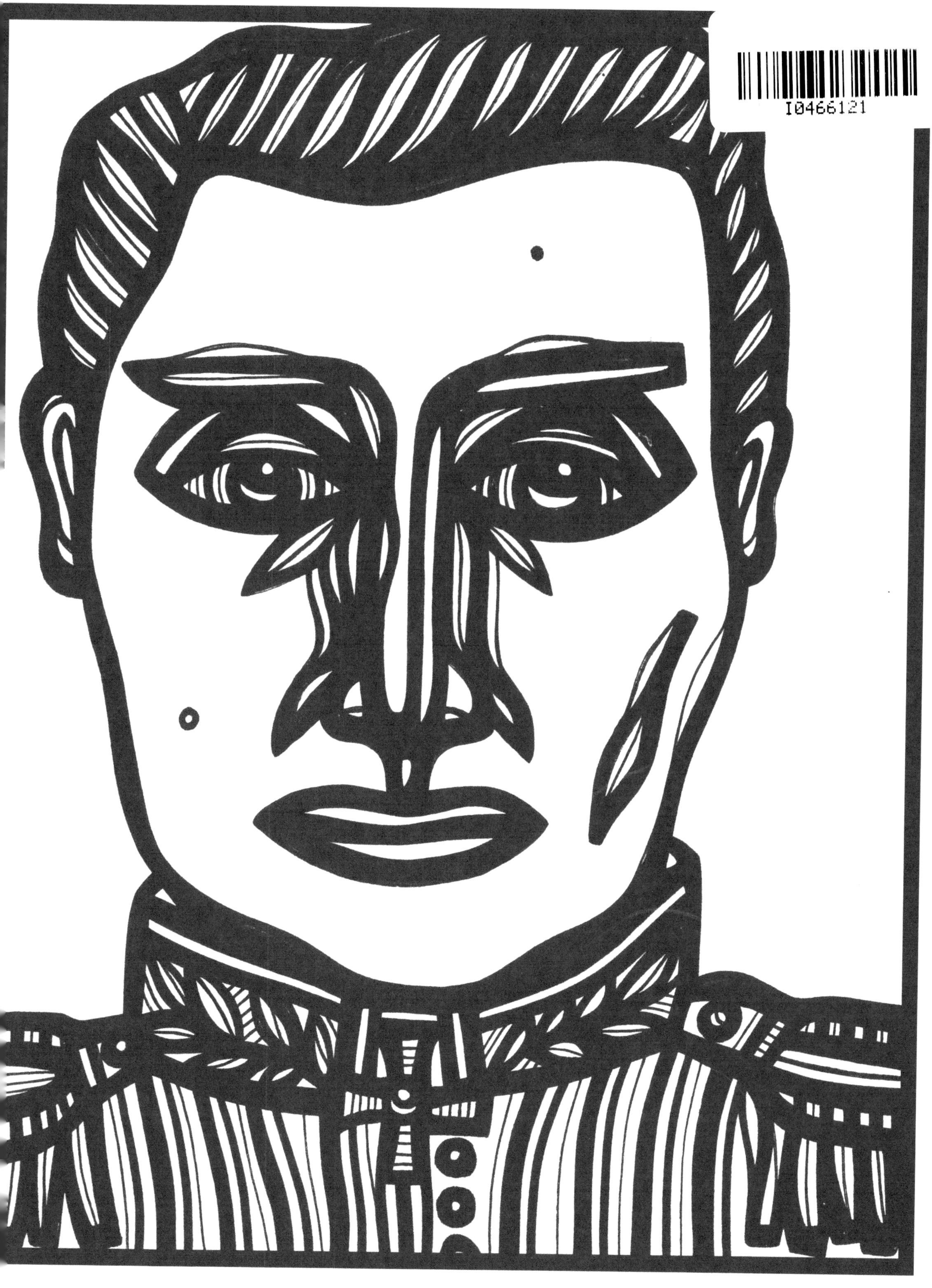

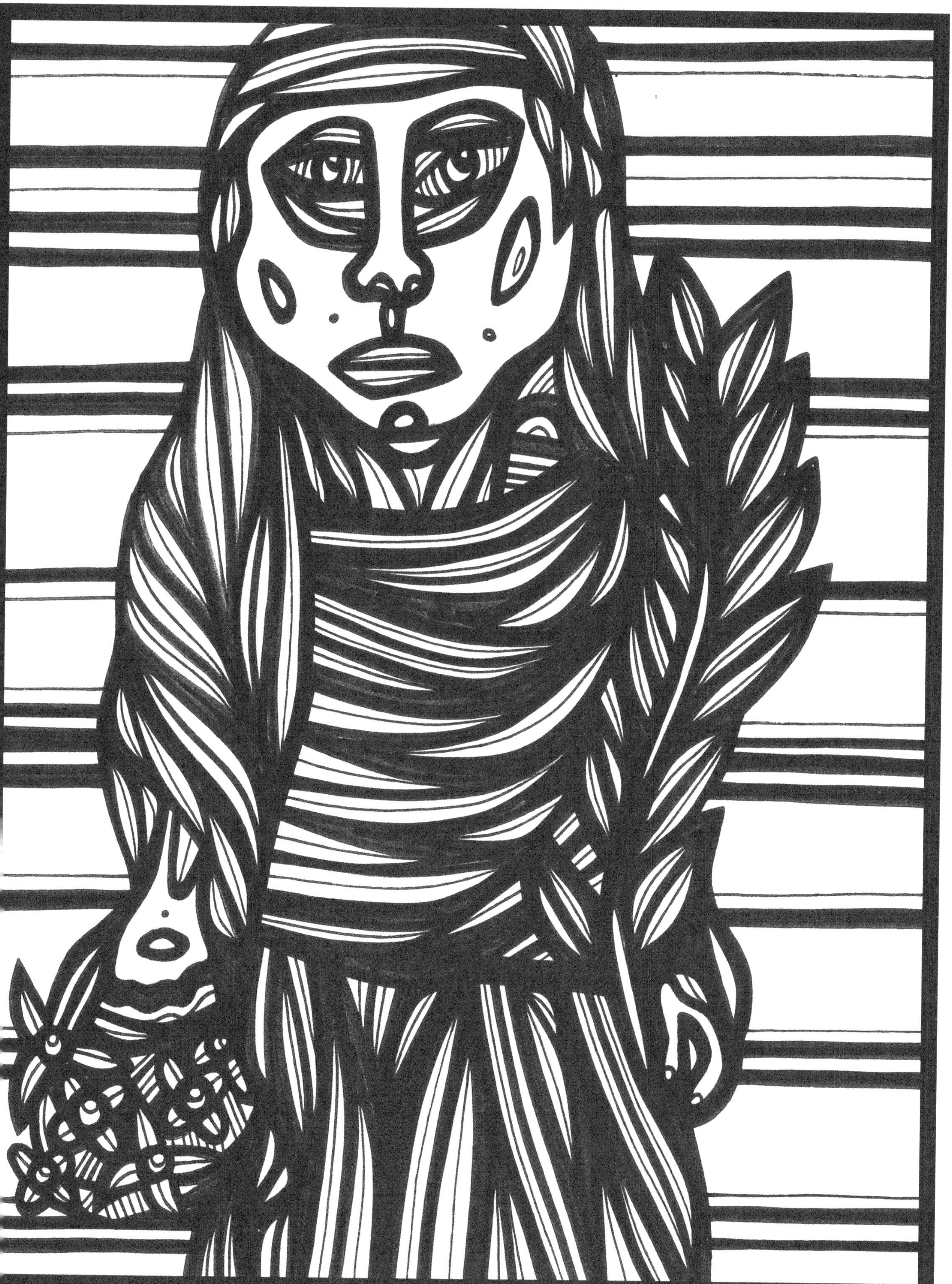

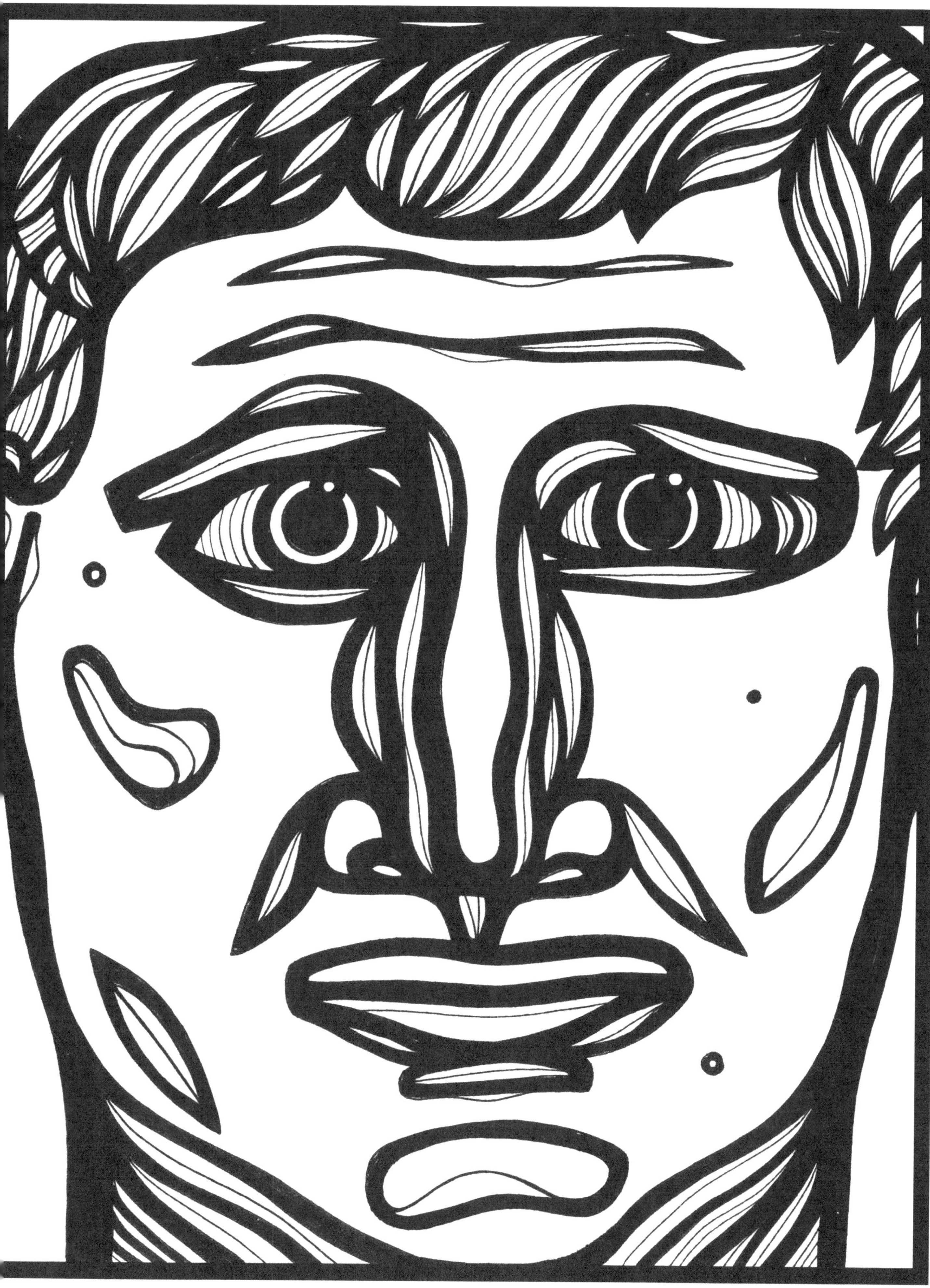

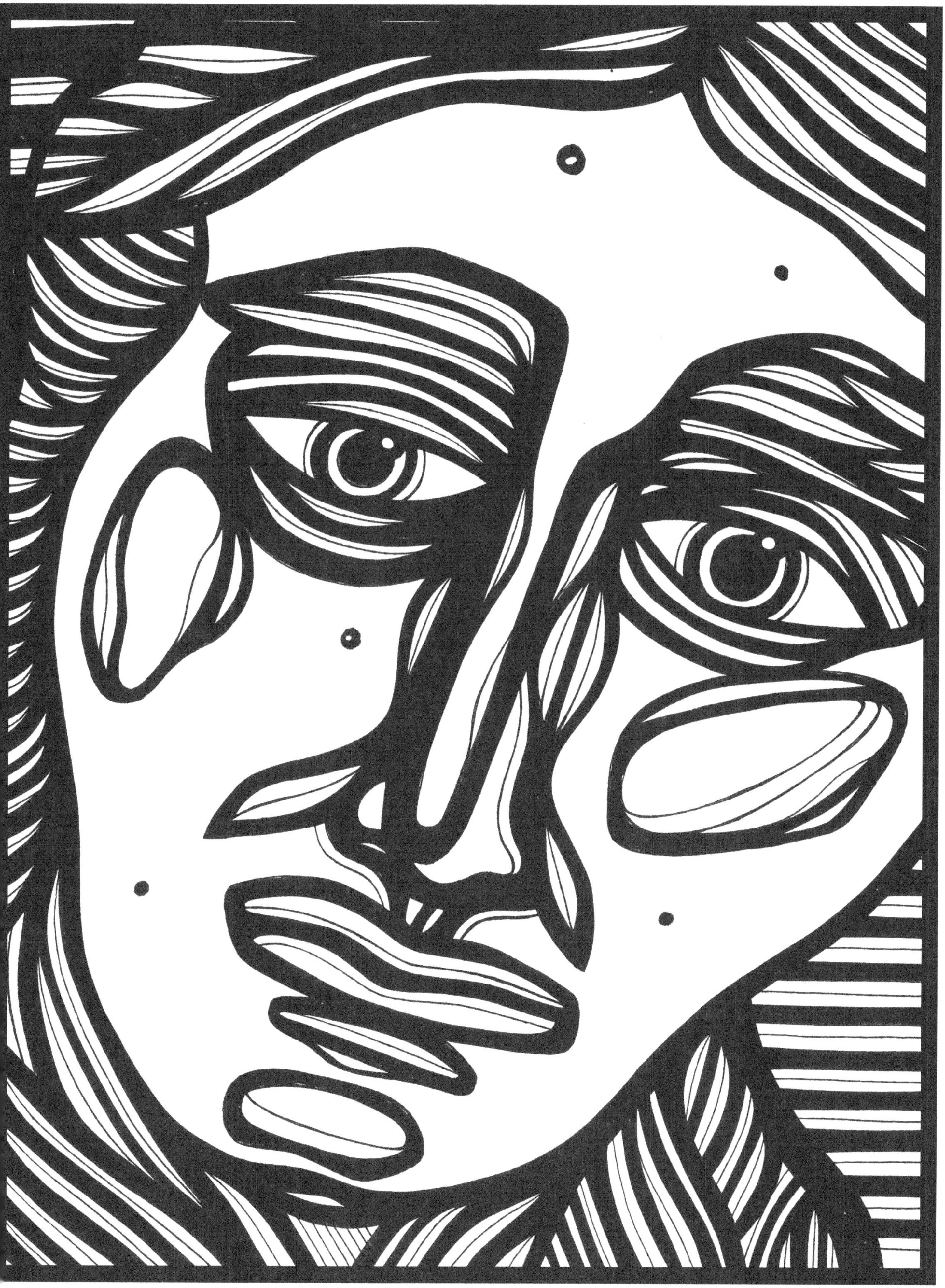

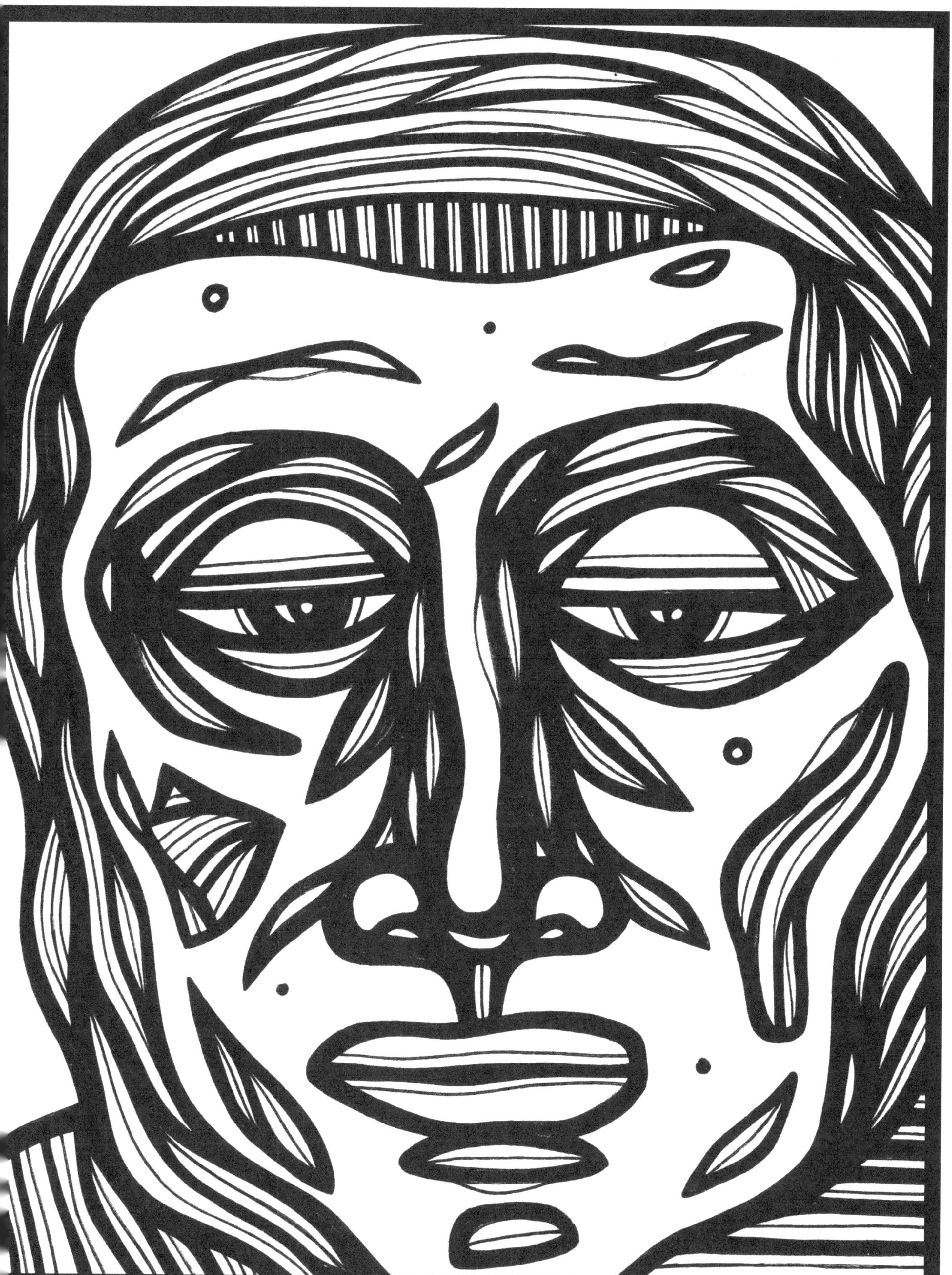

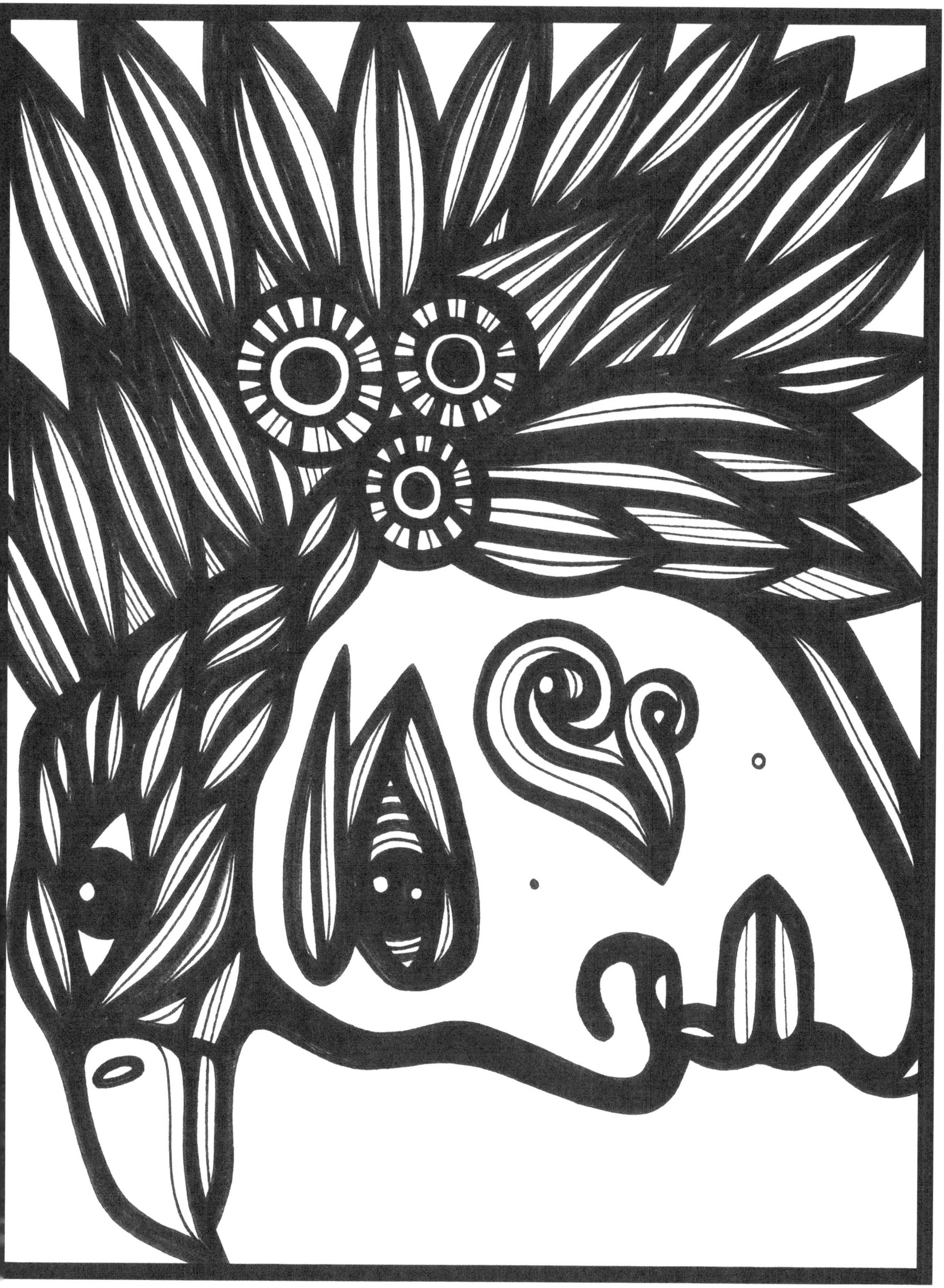

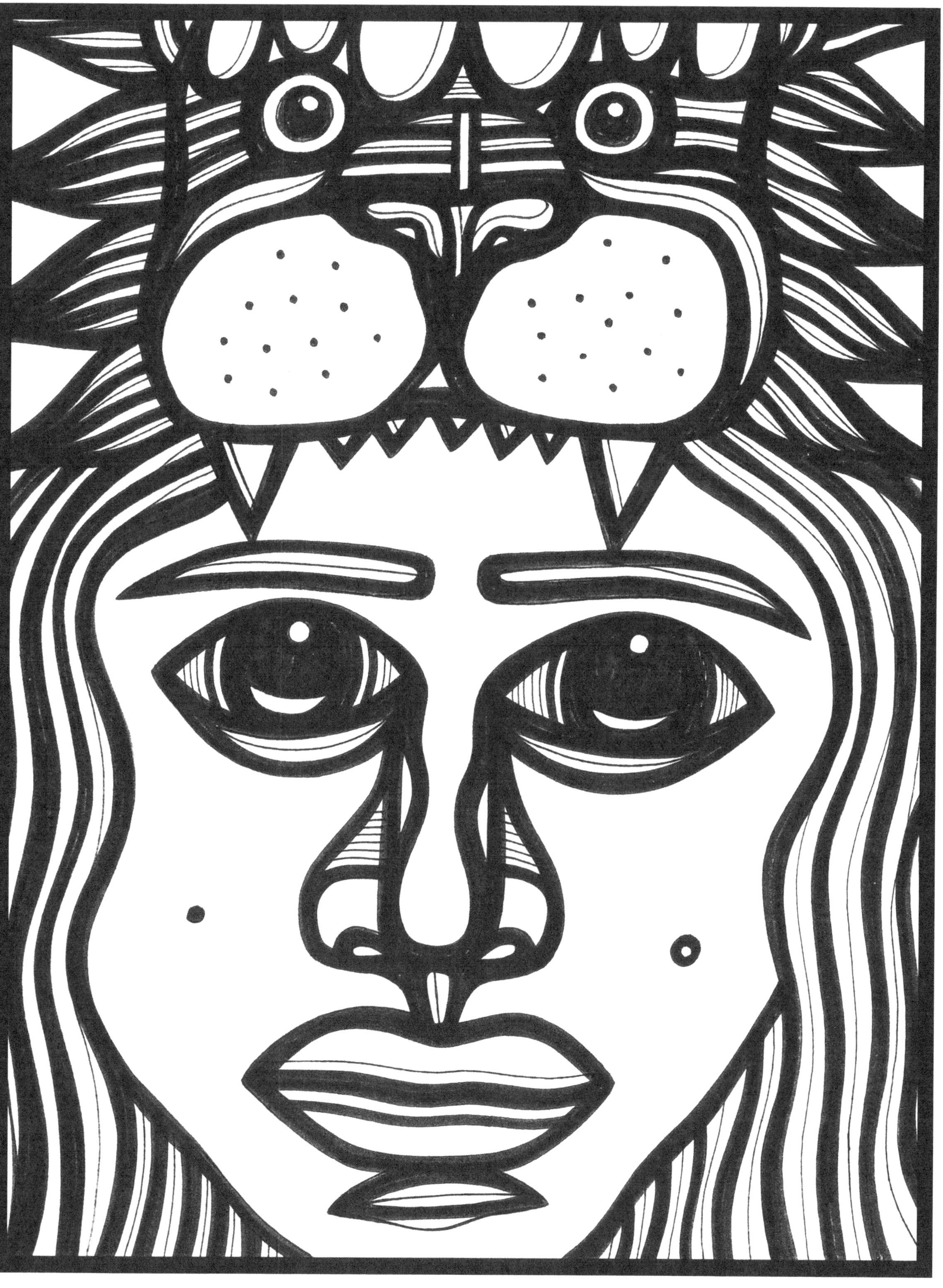

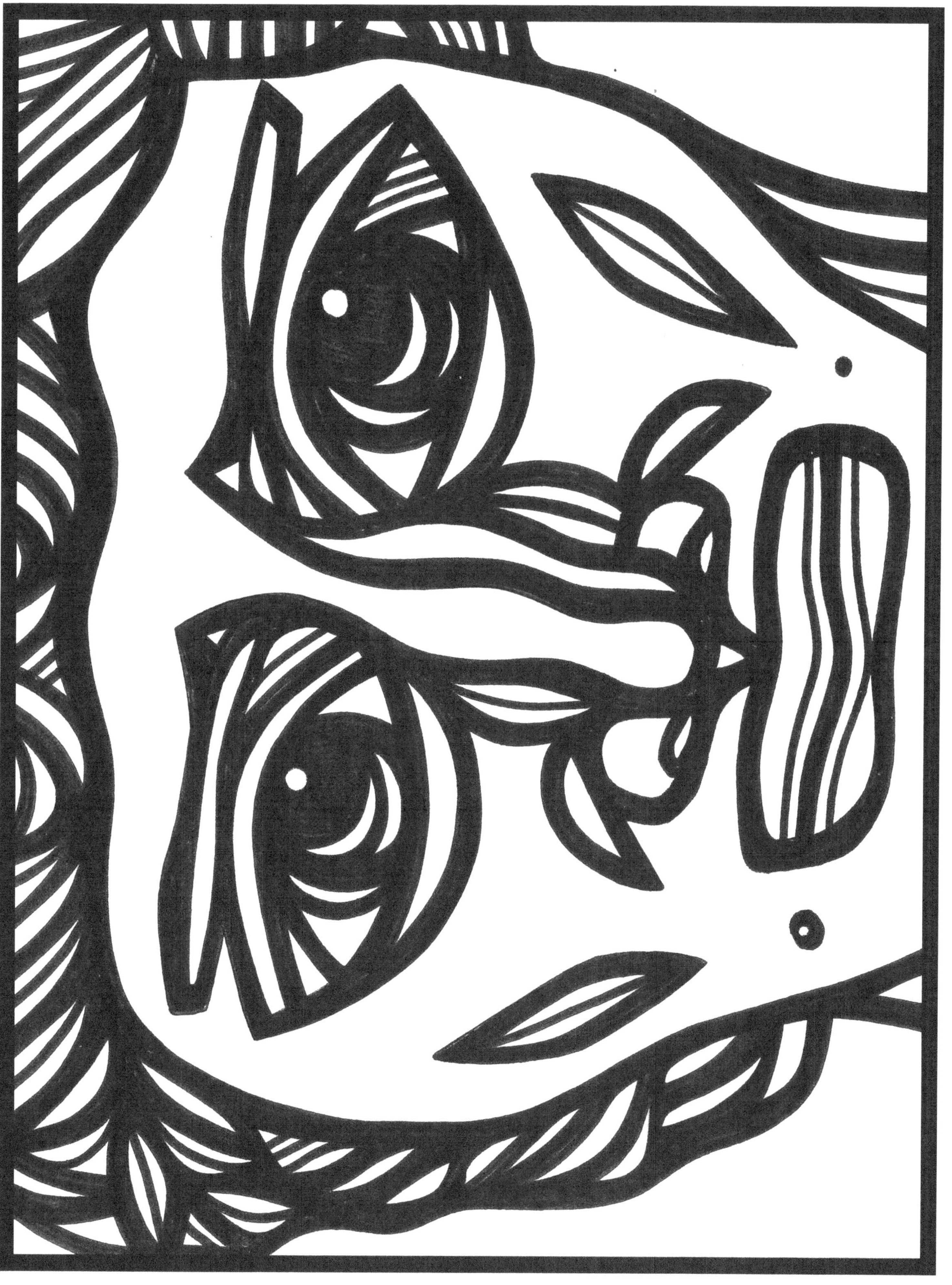

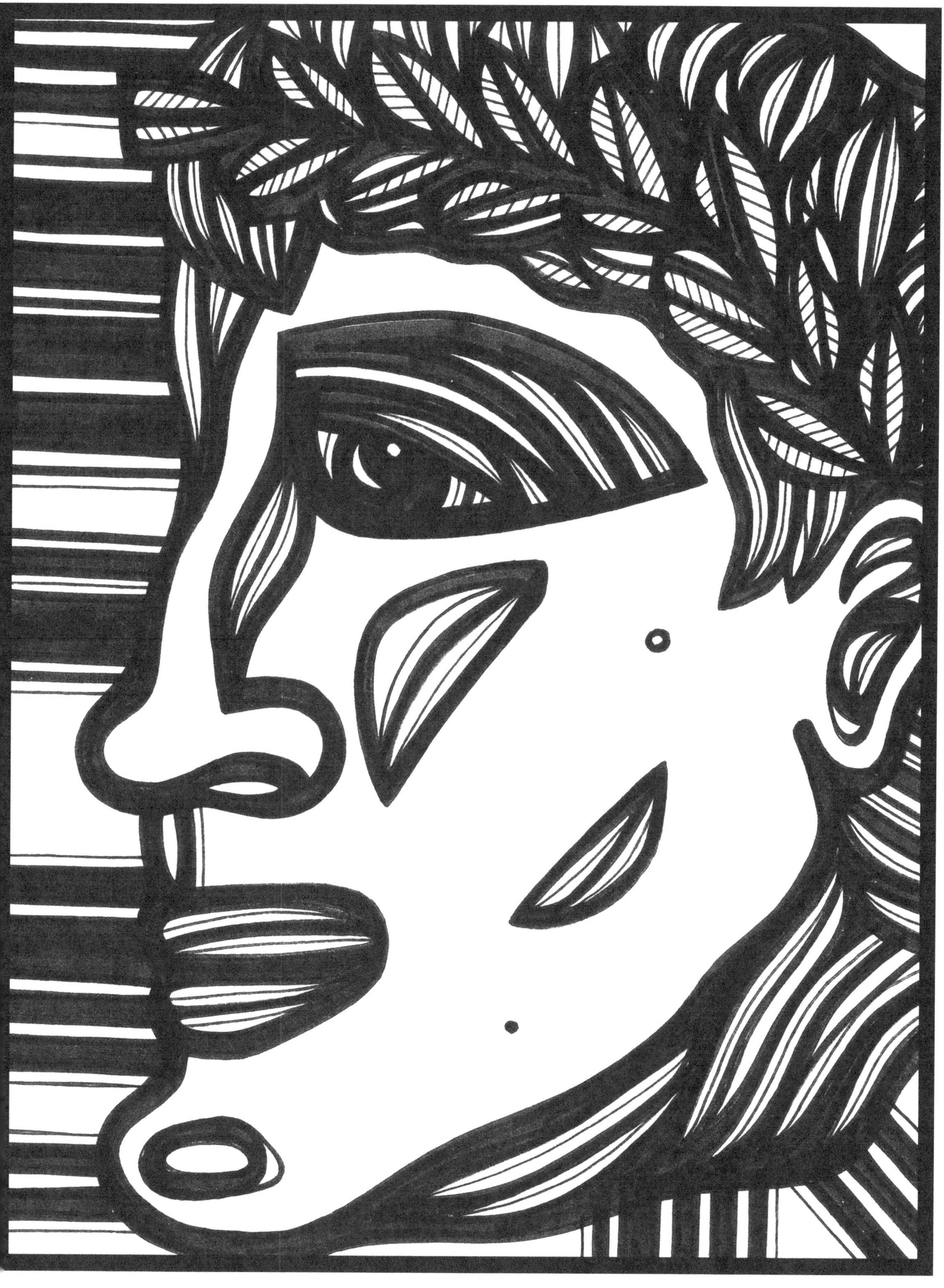

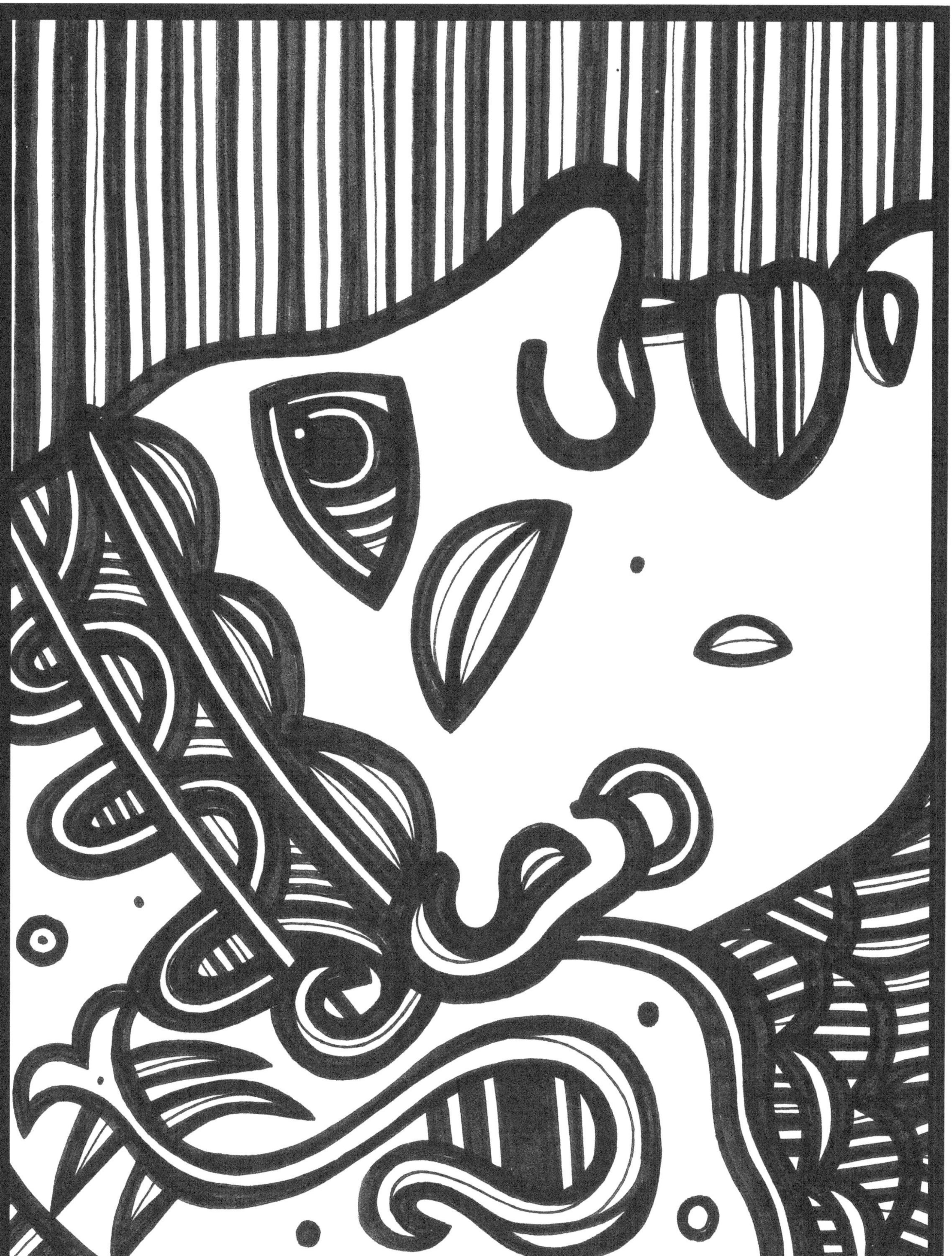

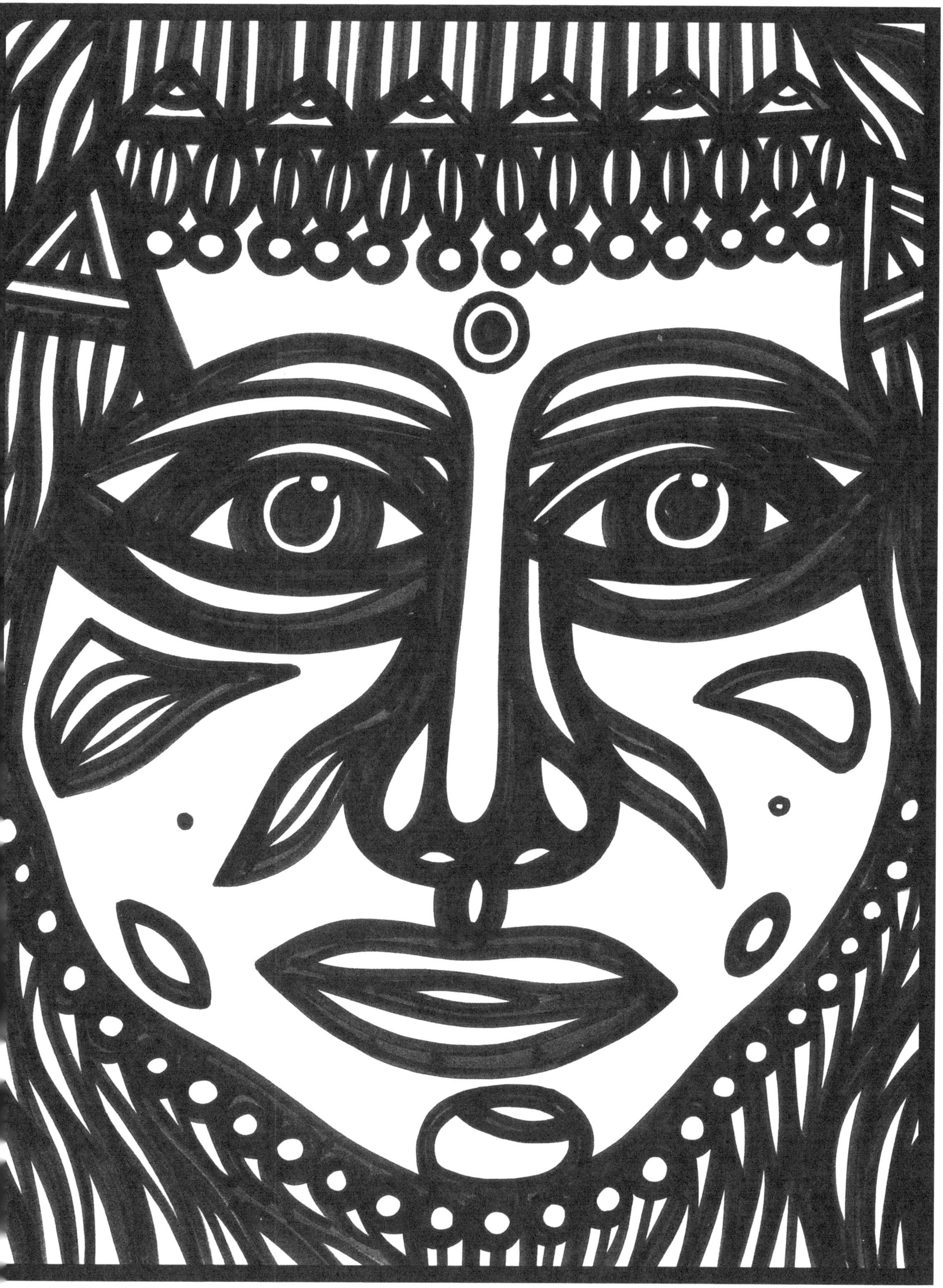

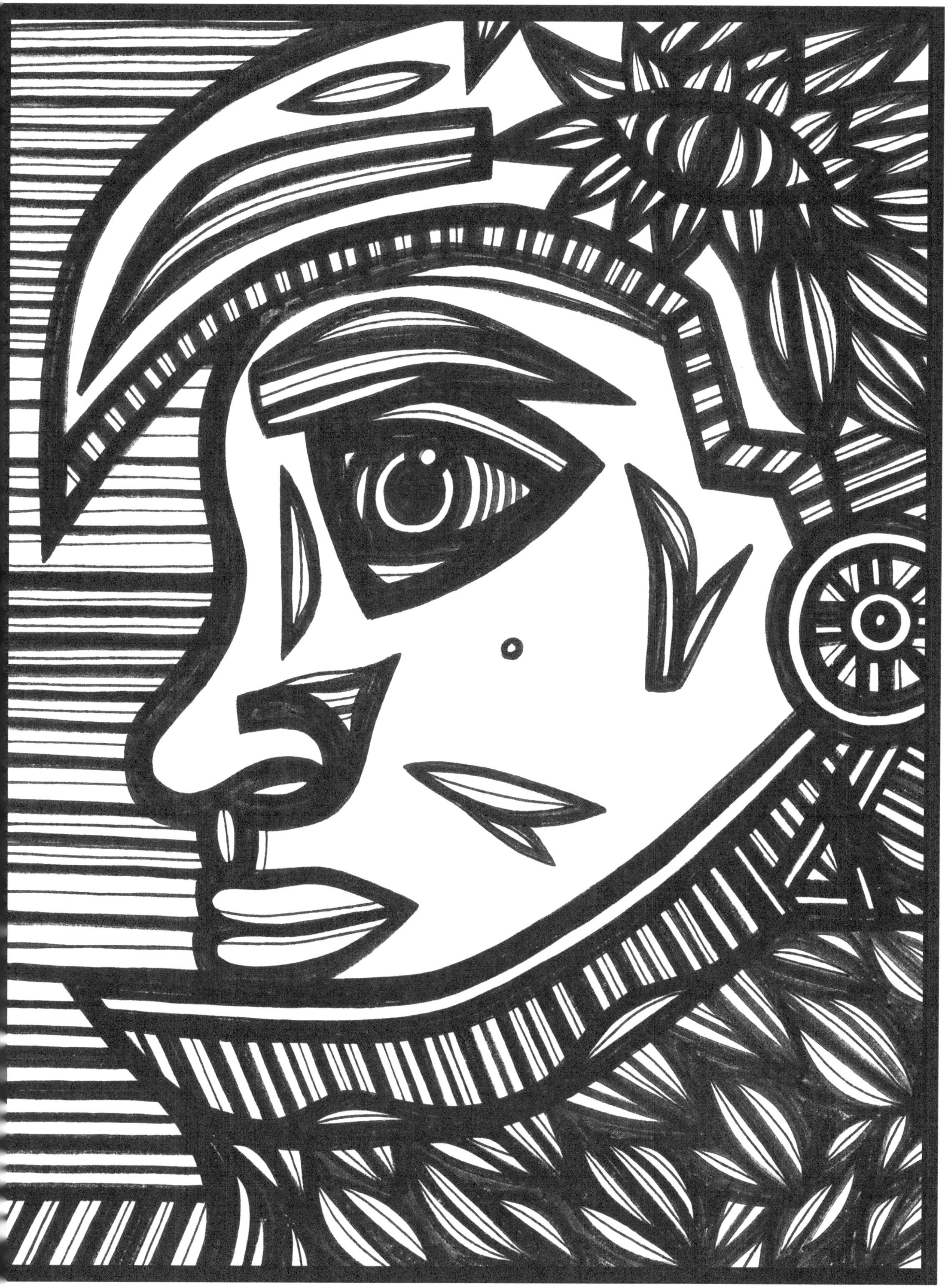

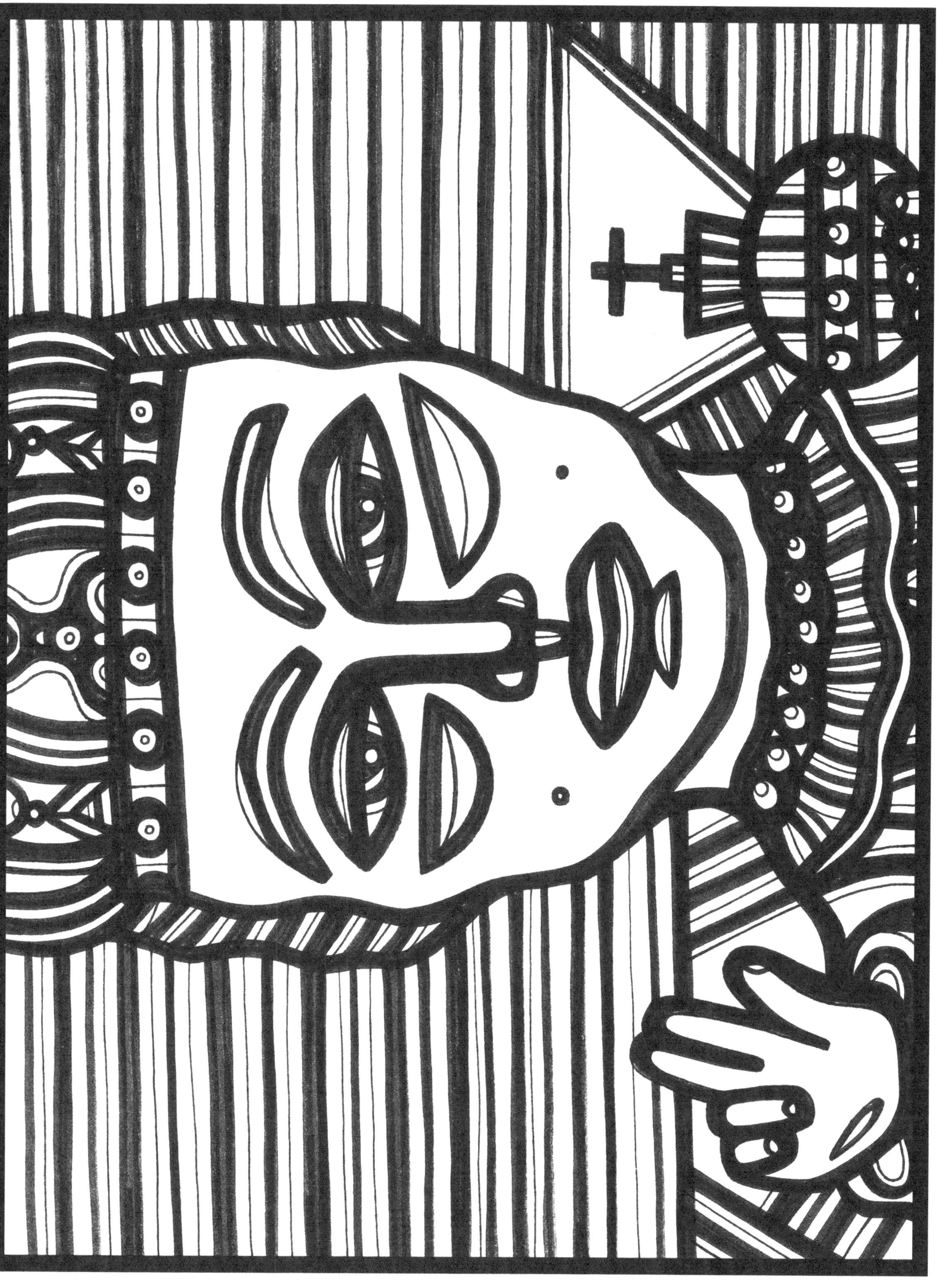

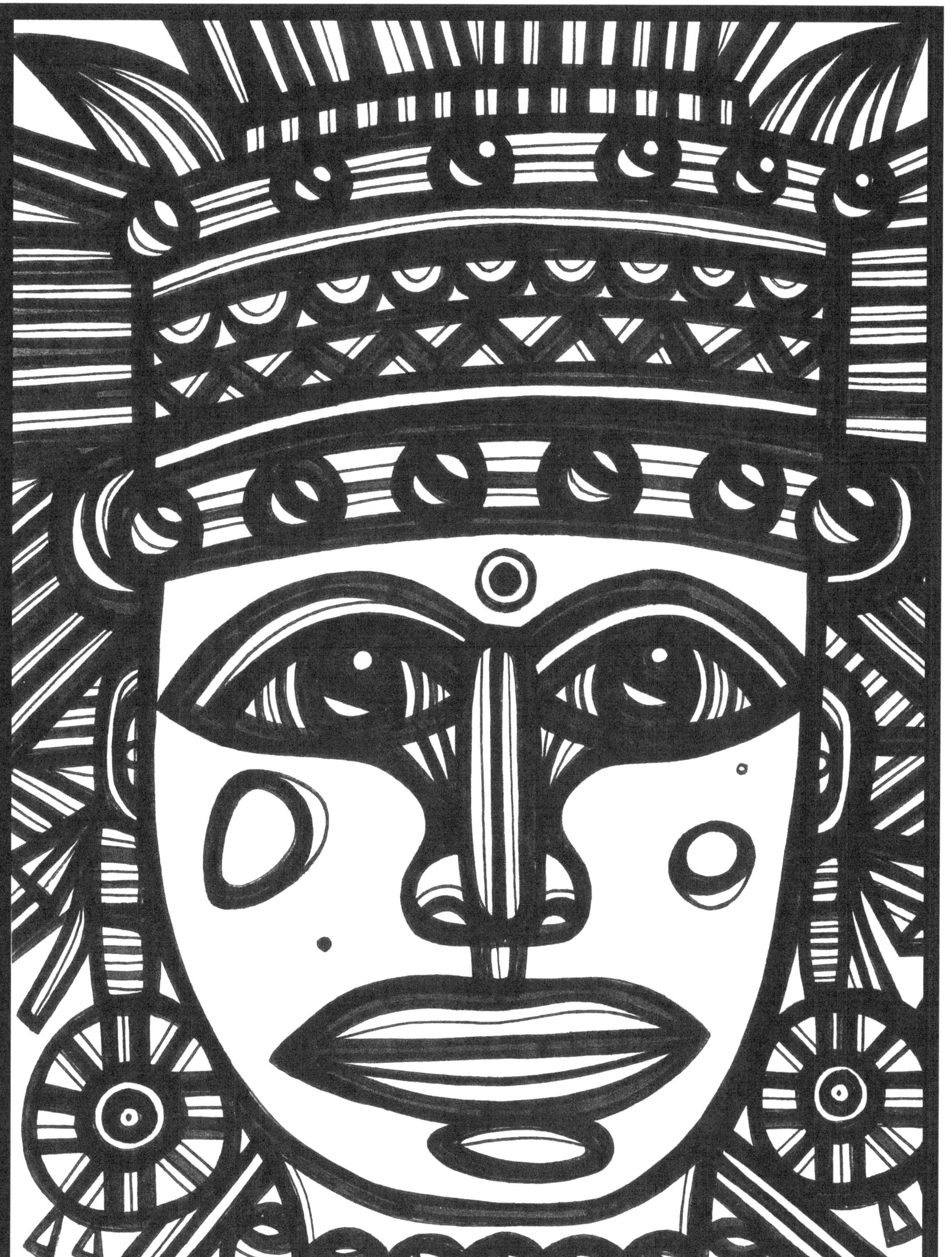

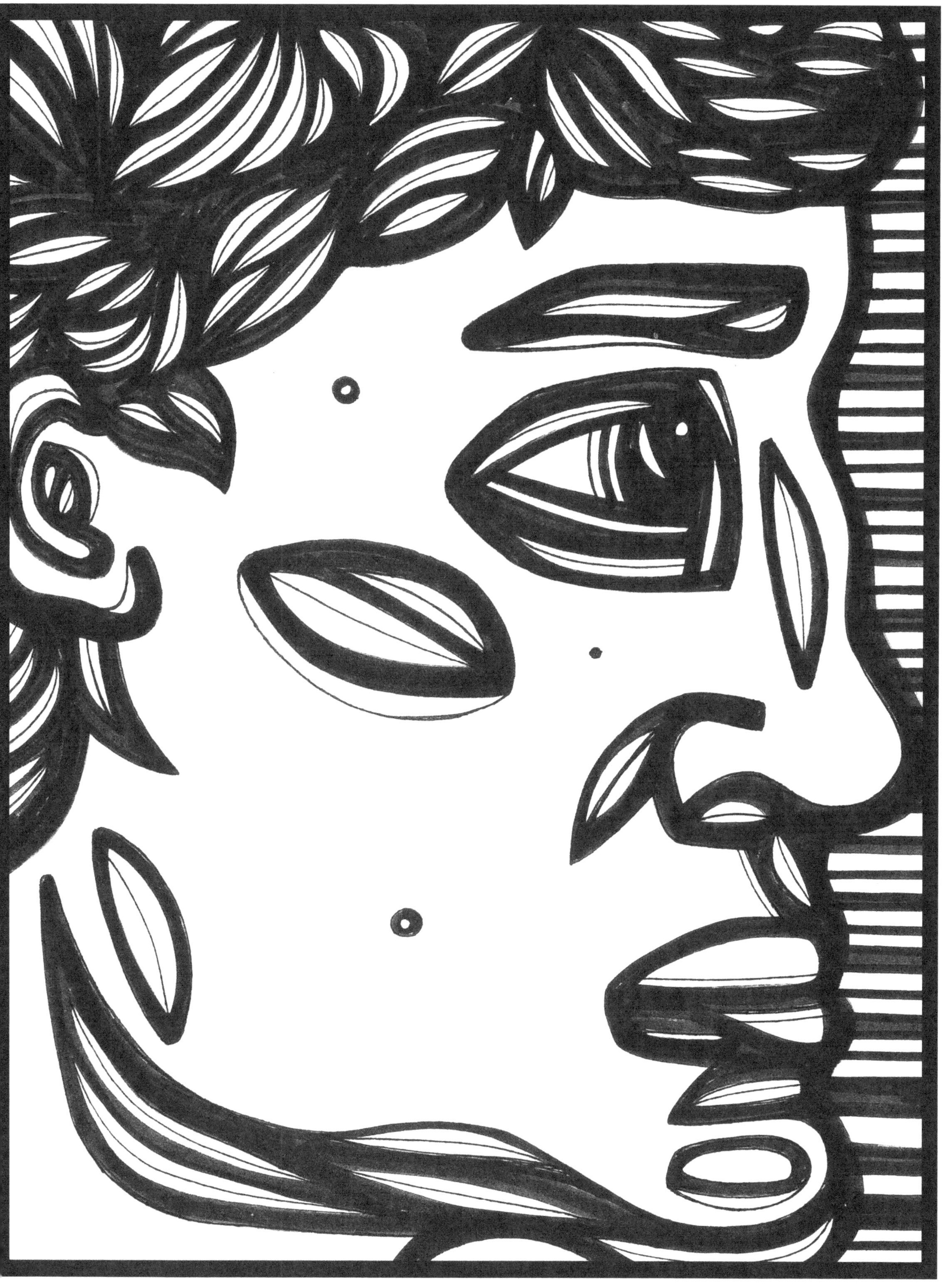

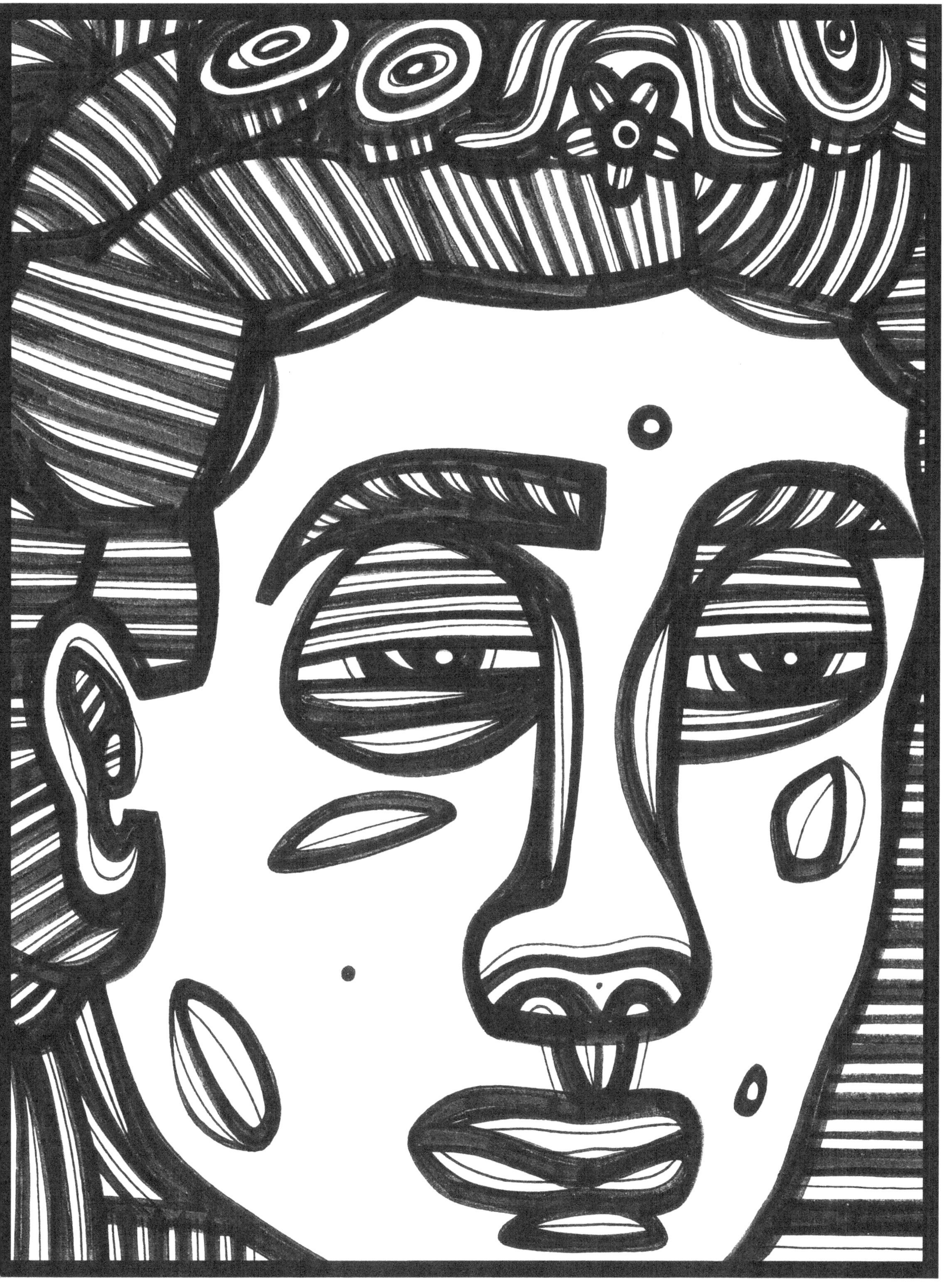

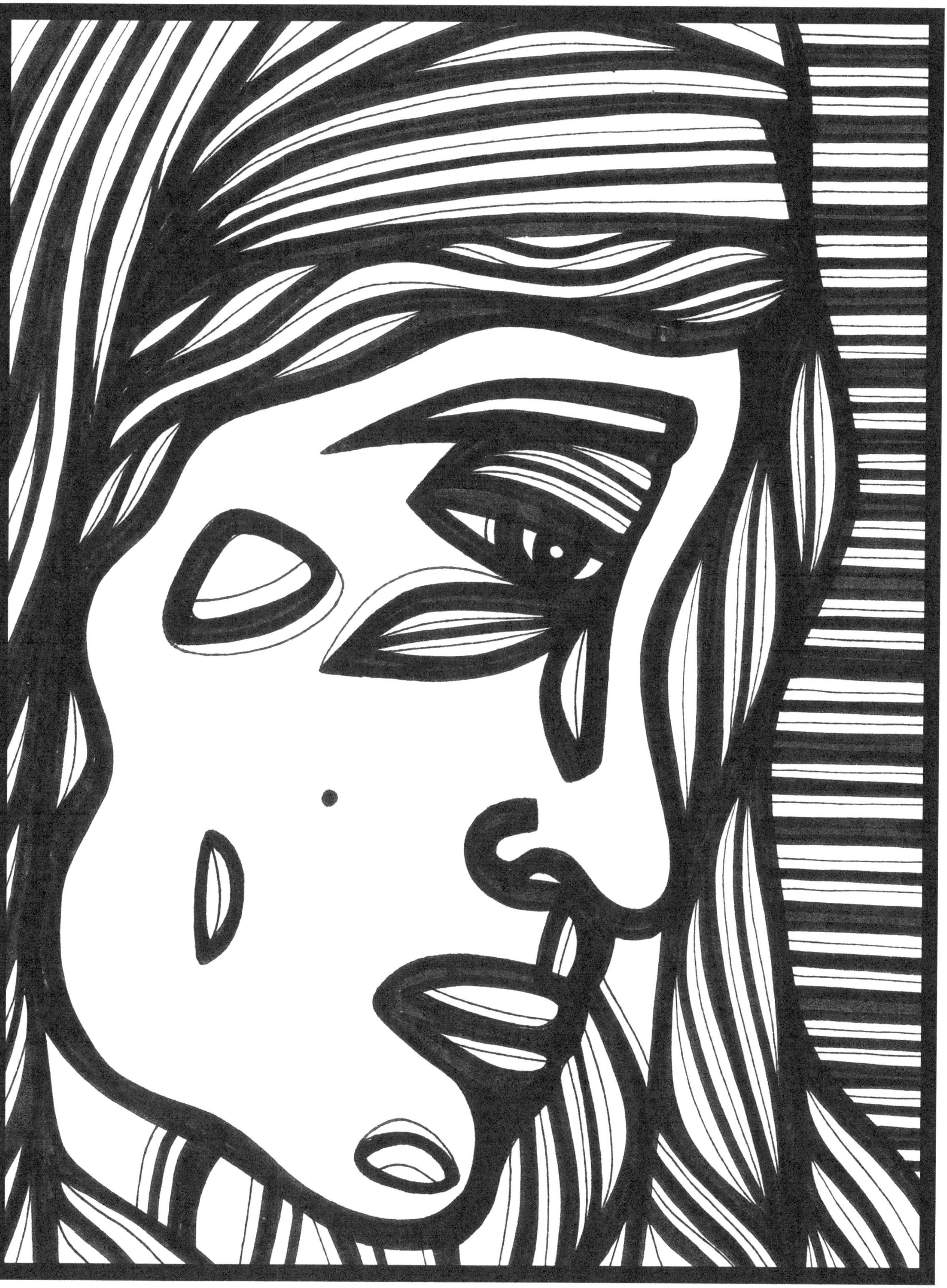

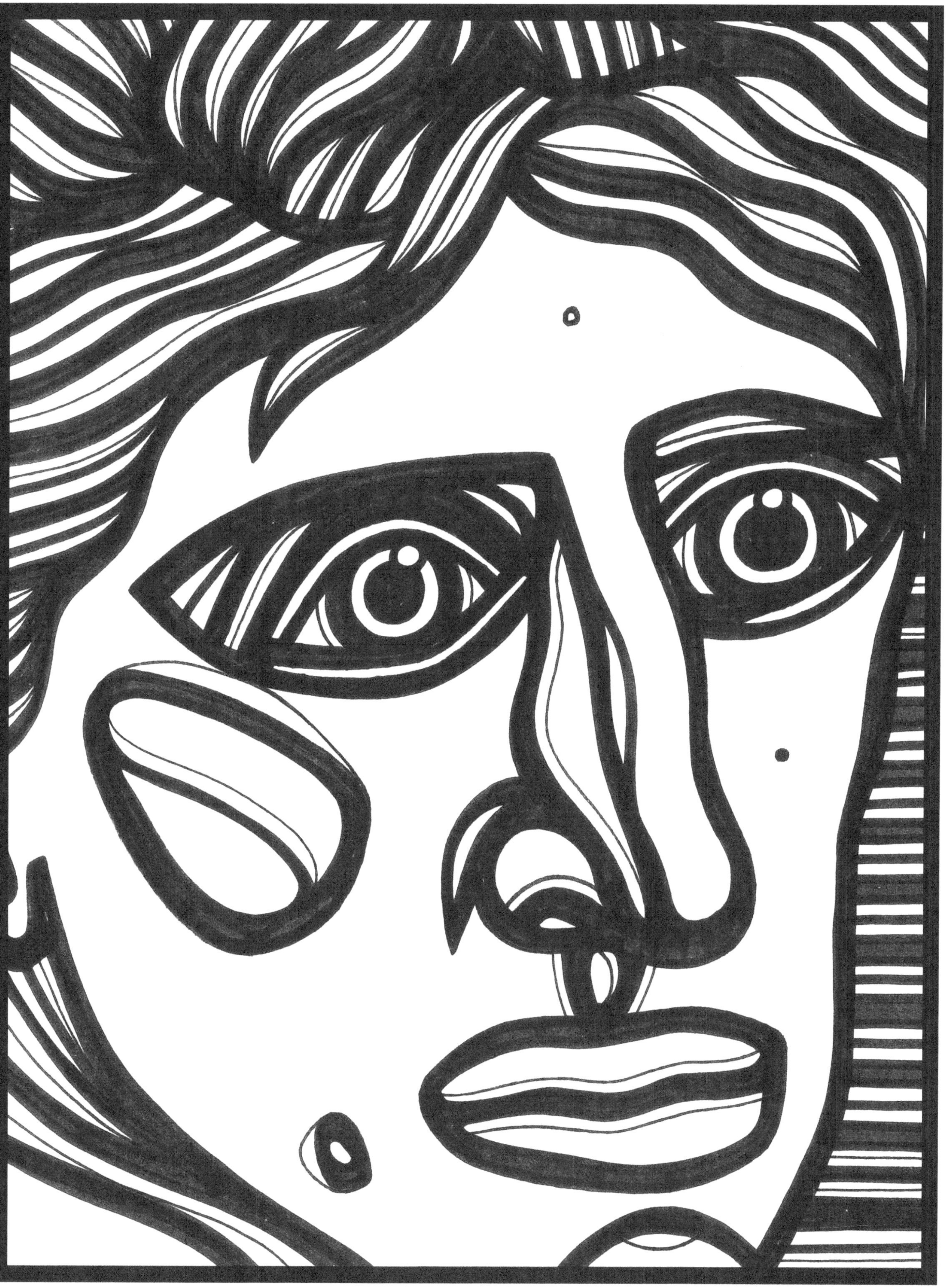

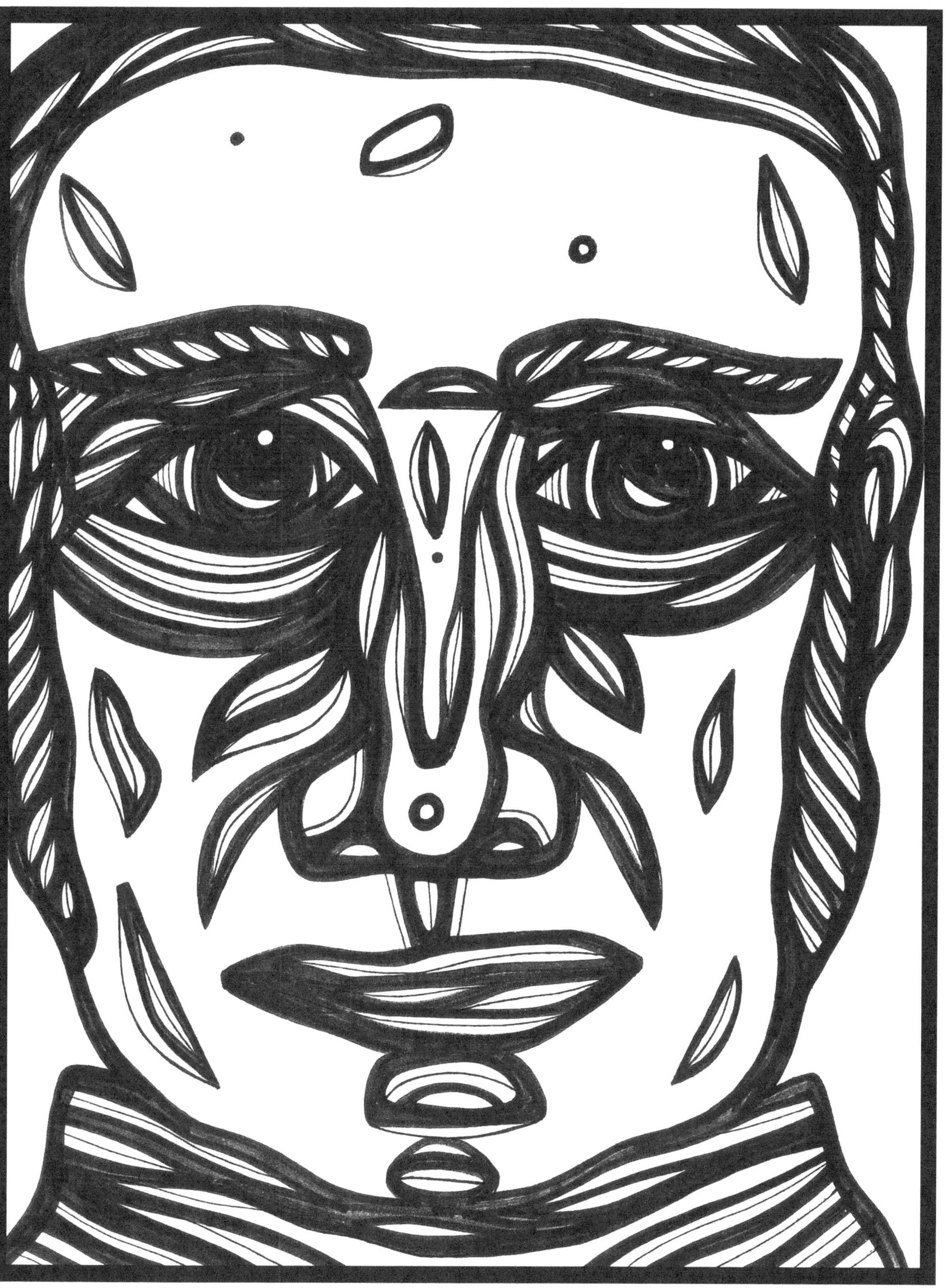

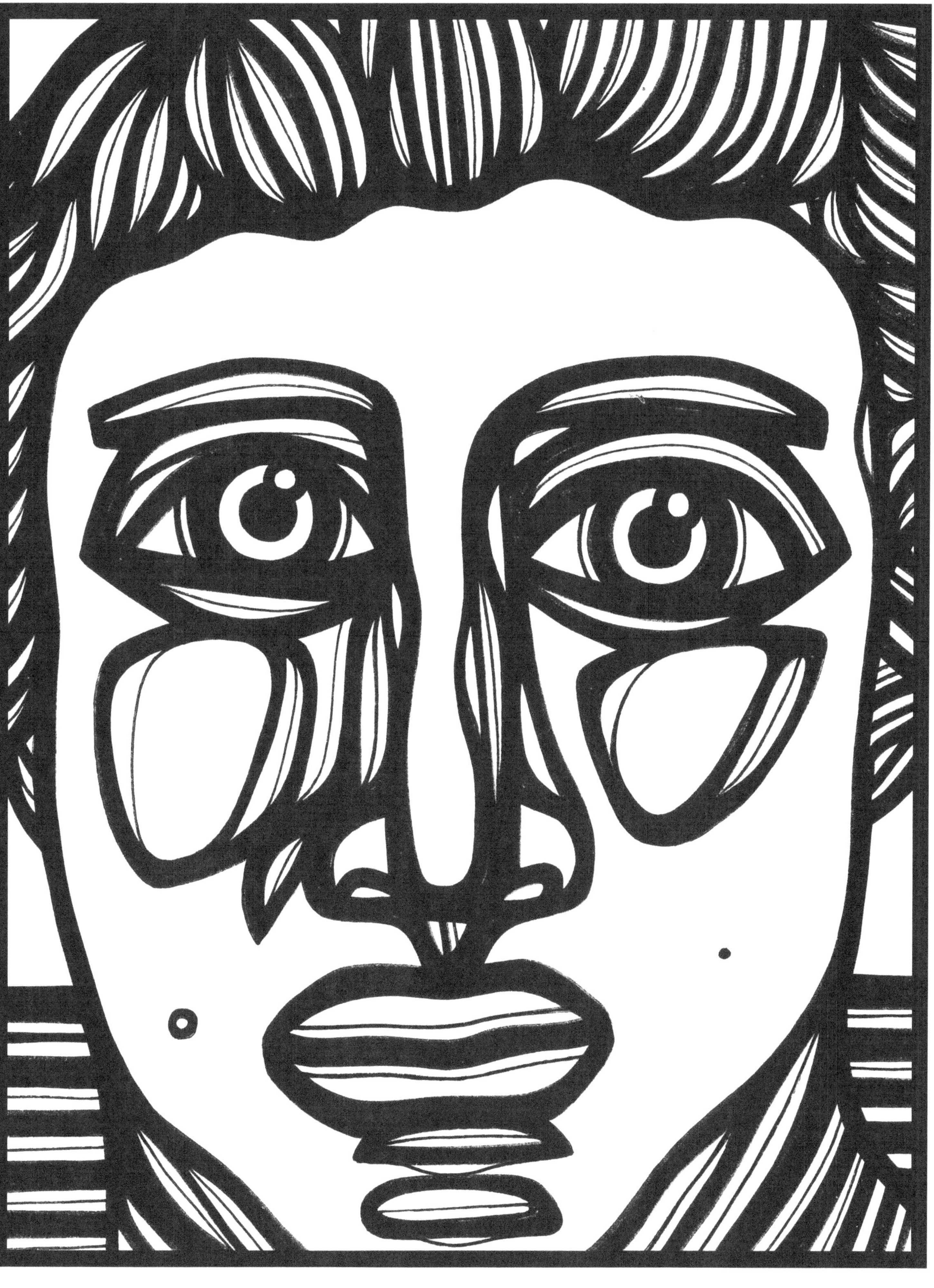

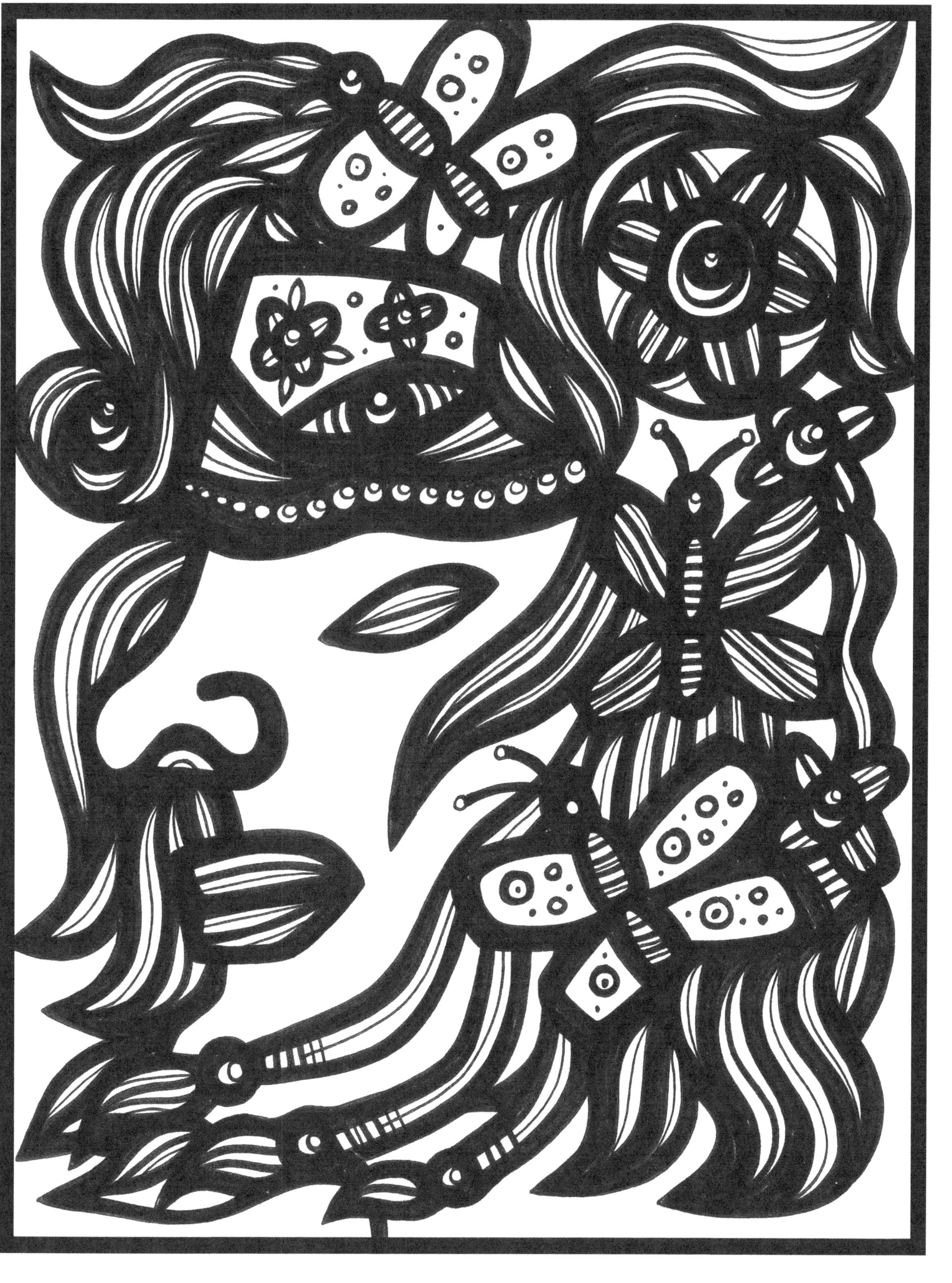

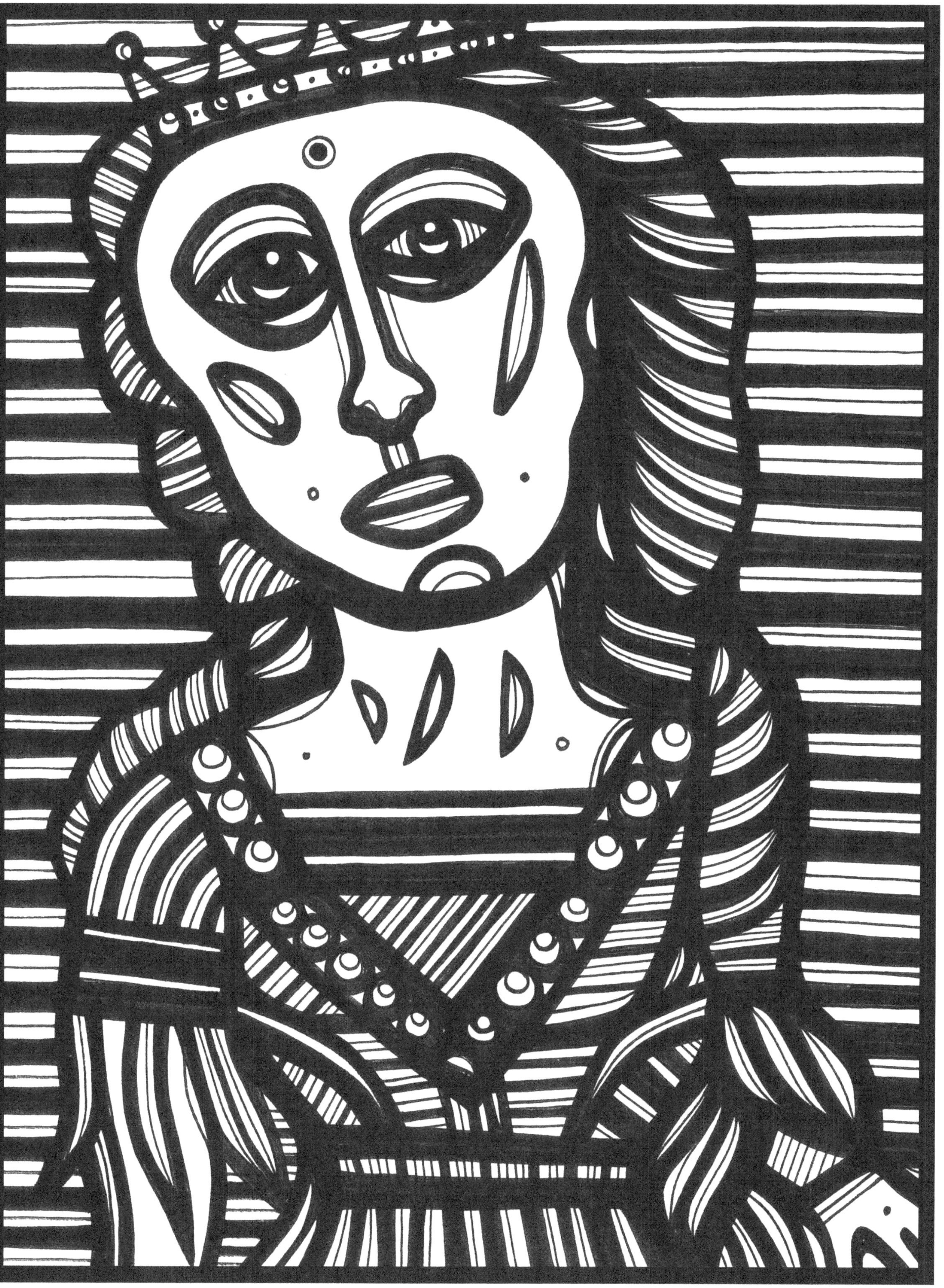

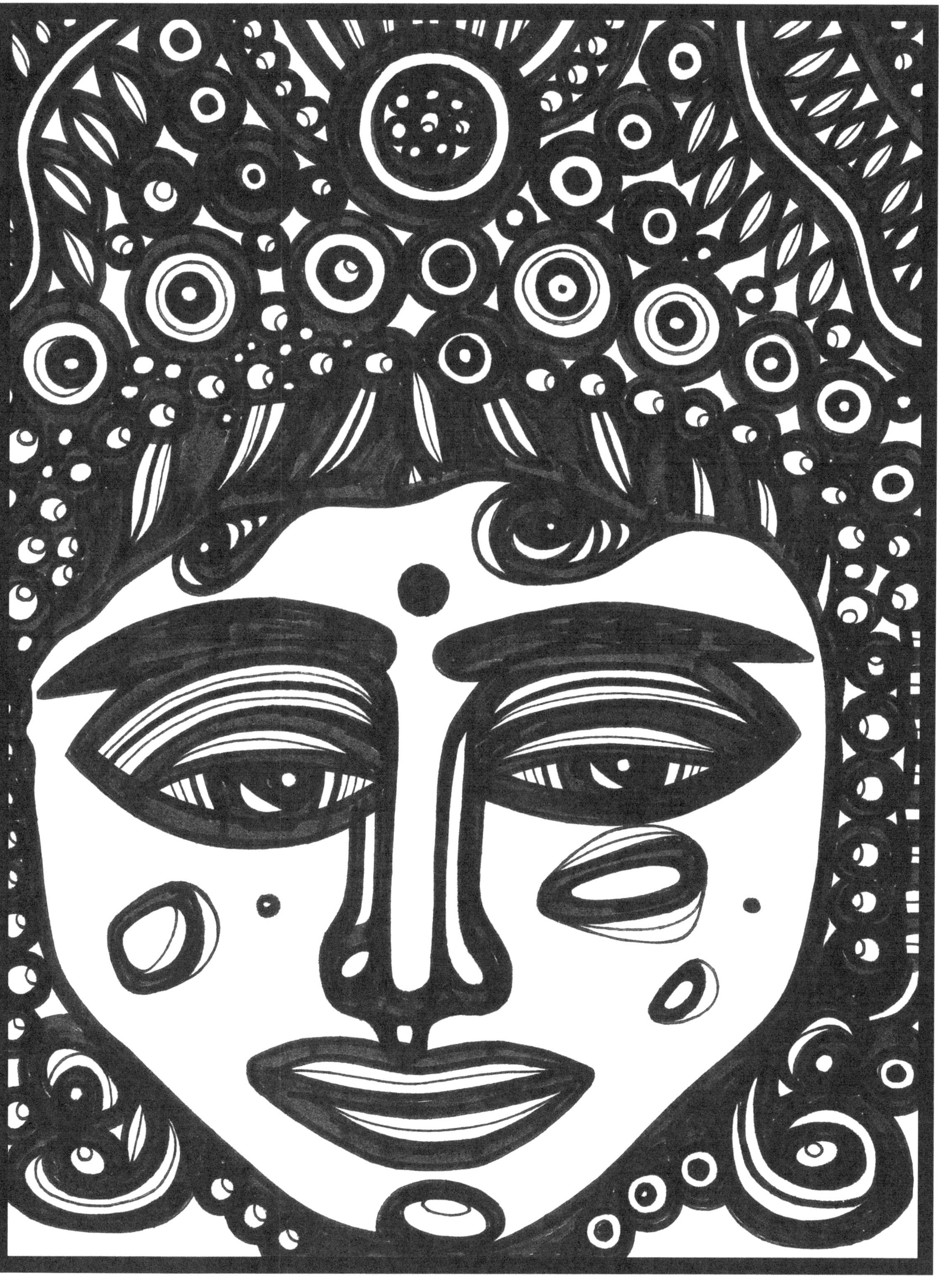

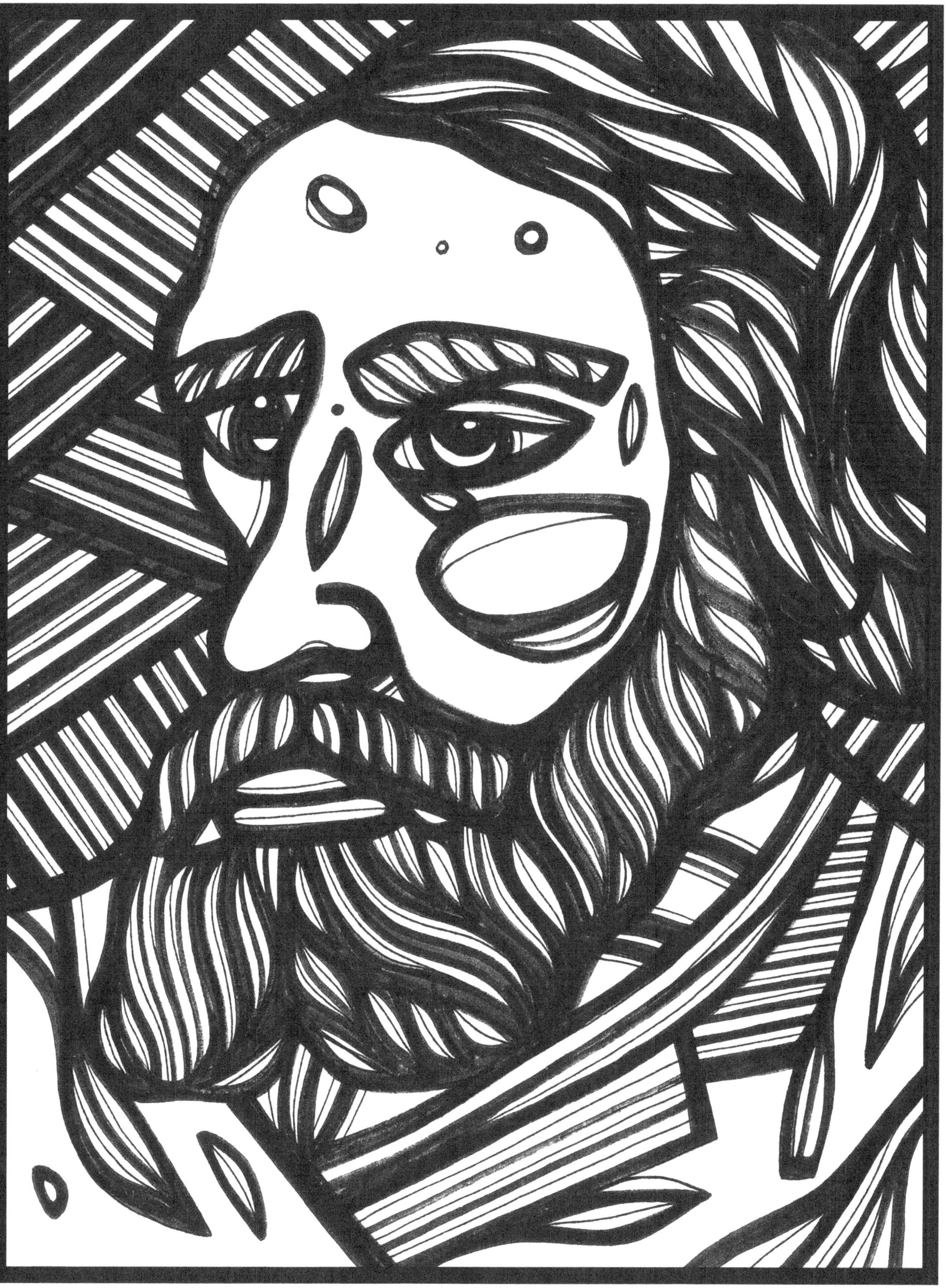

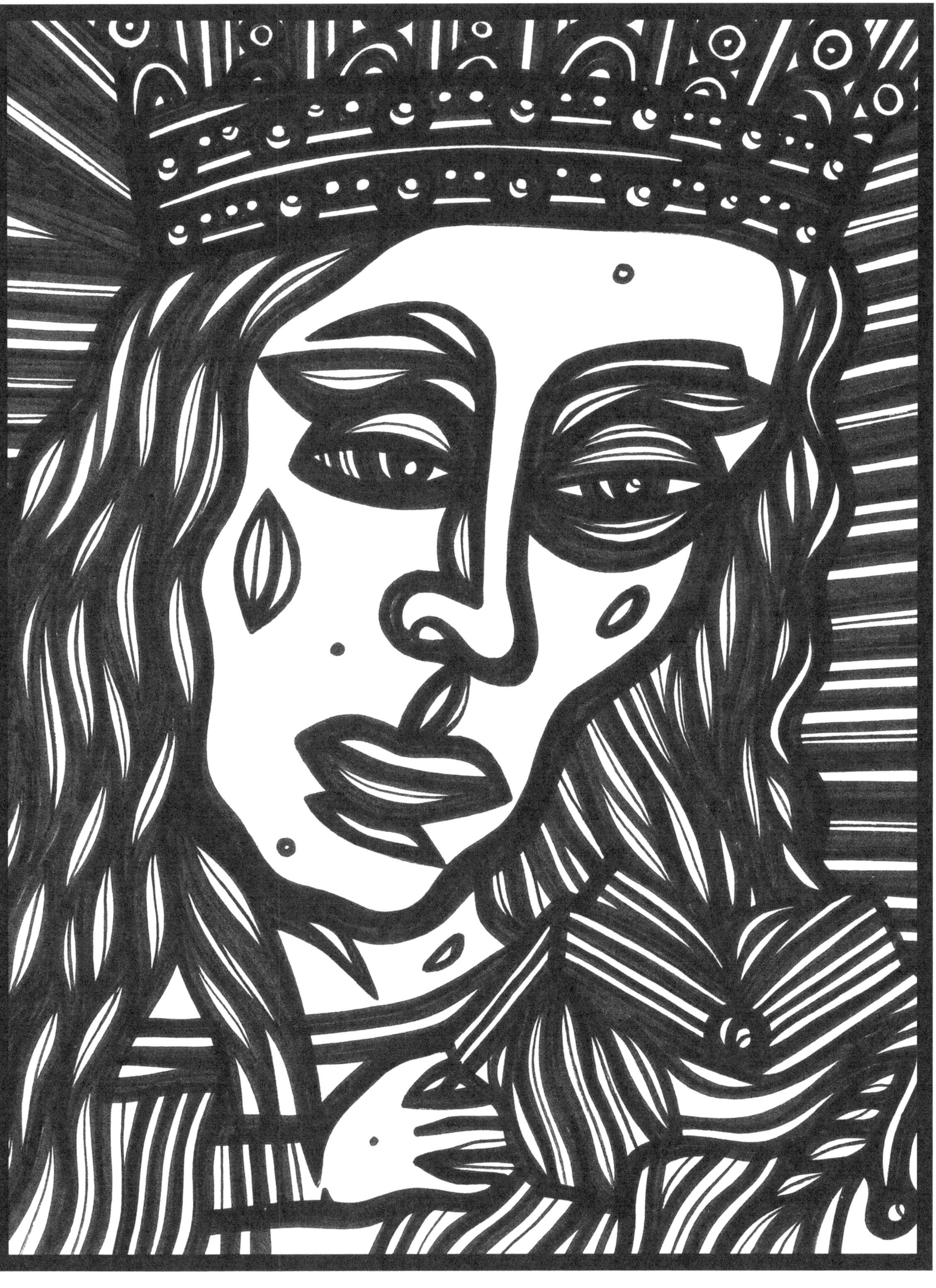

# THE END, THANK YOU.



MORE BOOKS:
631ART.COM

www.ingramcontent.com/pod-product-compliance
Lightning Source LLC
Chambersburg PA
CBHW080138240526
45468CB00009BA/2520
*9781795740890*